the RAWNESS of TIME

Ben Nuttall-Smith

The Rawness of Time

Copyright © Ben Nuttall-Smith 2022
Author: Ben Nuttall-Smith
Publisher: Rutherford Press
Author website: https://bennuttall-smith.ca
For information, contact:
    Rutherford Press,
    PO Box 648
    Qualicum Beach, BC, Canada V9K 1A0
    info@rutherfordpress.ca
    https://rutherfordpress.ca

Printed in the United States of America and Canada.

All rights reserved. No part of this book may be reproduced in whole or in part, materially or digitally, including photocopying, without the express written permission of the author or publisher.

ISBN   # 978-1-988739-52-6

Contents

TAP TAP 1

YOUR NAME 2

MONTREAL AIRPORT 3

COVID I 4

COVID II 5

COVID MASKS 6

THE MIGHTY CORONAVIRUS 7

MARTINIQUE 8

DOLPHINS 9

KAMIKAZE 10

SUNDAY IN MARTINIQUE 11

QUELLE PATIENCE! 14

AS A FATHER SHOULD BE 15

DRIVING WITH MY FATHER 16

MARTINIQUE RUM 17

SUMAS LAKE, BRITISH COLUMBIA 18

SNOW 19

GARDENS 20

STONES & DRIFTWOOD 22

GARDEN PLANTS	23
THE CULPABILITY OF VALERIA	24
MY MOTHER'S GARDEN	26
FRIENDS IN MY GARDEN	28
MARGOT'S GARDEN	29
GOLD DUST & BLACK DEATH	30
THIS YEAR'S GARDEN	31
BOOZE, BREAKUP AND COUNSELLING	32
WE HAUNT THE PAST	36
I SHALL RETURN	37
LISTENING	38
THE IRIS	39
PARENTHOOD	40
GRANDCHILDREN	41
FISH AND CHIPS	42
MISSION	45
GUILT	46
AND A CHILD WILL LEAD	47
PRAYER	48
KARMA	49
THE SHAWL	50

DISOWNED – DISINHERITED	54
RULED BY GREED	55
HIDDEN	56
BIRTH	57
VALCARTIER, QUEBEC	59
VICTIM	60
WAR AND HEALING	62
EARLIEST MEMORIES	63
REMEMBERING AND LETTING GO	64
A WARTIME STORY	65
THE SECRET	70
DEALING WITH A QUIZLING	76
CLOSING THOUGHTS	85
AFTER I'M GONE	86

From the Editor

A person of advanced years will have developed a certain perspective on the events that have brought him or her to that point.

One tends to shred away unimportant things and to dwell on what it was that has moulded one's character. As such, a senior's thoughts become the most personal of spaces. It takes, perhaps, reckless courage to expose those distilled memories for others to examine. Only a small number of *survivors into elderhood* will bother with, or be brave enough to, open up one's soul in as much of a raw fashion as does Ben in these poems and recollections.

He wishes to state with respect that some of his memories about his deeply enigmatic mother may not correspond to what others remember. Ben is apologetic. He only wishes to know more.

with love,
George Opacic,
January 2022

TAP TAP

The muscles in his legs
have withered in the chill
of long flown years.
Tap, tap his cane
against the crumbling stone
of steps he once laid down,
so long ago, the memory's gone,
he'd set the two-foot wall
to hold his blossoms firm
and plucked a bouquet
almost every morn
for one who made the days so warm.
She left before the wilted leaves
had blown and fading roses
withered on the bower.
And so tap tap, he waits his turn
to join her one day
in the great unknown.

YOUR NAME

The face I know so well,

hello again, dear friend.

Sorry if I don't recall your name

when daily you greet me by mine.

Thick cobwebs gather

where my thoughts once flew.

But now, like flies,

they buzz in the maze.

MONTREAL AIRPORT

2:30 A.M.

Waiting on a hard bench

a very hard bench

sleepless.

We'd been led to the inner exit

in error no doubt

to clear the hallways.

However

warm dry safe

Many lodge on damp cardboard

in shop doorways

night after endless night

cold hungry alone

"There but for fortune …"

COVID I

Every now and then,

to even up the score,

Mother Nature signals

"That's enough!"

and creatures

far too small for us to see

but mightier than all the armies

sent by men in war

come forth to stop us

in our plunder

and our greed.

They almost succeed.

COVID II

From morn to night and then again

in travel crowds we shield our breath

with gauze that tugs and pulls our ears

and mists our glasses should we try to read.

How precious is the air we share

while Nature's unseen creatures lurk

to haunt the streams of life

which trees and ocean plants

send out as gifts.

Shall we destroy these too?

COVID MASKS

Faces we can no longer recognize.

The clothing? The voice? We must surmise.

We see black or white or medicinal blue,

we could be in Moose Jaw or Timbuktu.

We display a new invisibility

as we furtively shuffle within our municipality.

Some choose to sneak over the parapet with an open nose,

and some scoff at science, preferring chance, I suppose.

In this new time of dreadful sameness, how to be an individual?

With a hat, a scarf, a laugh to escape the covid mantle?

As anxious lethargy passes on to torpor,

is that a cousin or my next door neighbour?

Are those lines of masked mugs waiting for a jab?

Or have they forsaken the bus and await a cab?

I've finally discovered what my mother did not ascertain

that shaving or makeup lies unseen behind the filter curtain

and to avoid an encounter with a tree

by tilting my-glasses to some degree

I can avoid the blasted fog!

THE MIGHTY CORONAVIRUS

Man is but a speck in the history of creation. By brutal strength we have placed ourselves at the helm of what we are about to destroy. We write histories to lend credence to the myth that we are the sole reason for Creation that is, by its very nature, an ongoing process. The seven days have passed. What now?

The tiniest birds mate and build relationships, caring one for the other, often for life. They do not divorce. Porpoises live together in huge families, selecting leaders and watching out for one another. Wolves run in coordinated packs. Even trees communicate, reaching out through their roots for mutual support. Elephants and crows mourn their dead. The ant still follows paths set down millions of years ago.

Only people take more than could ever be used. The world is ruled by greed.

We have created God in our own image, sometimes loving, too often angry and destructive. We are the only creatures that wilfully destroy not only one another but the very environment upon which all life depends.

Perhaps by the tiniest of creatures we, too, will be destroyed.

MARTINIQUE

Island of pale-skinned sun-kissed tourists,

ebony Martiniquais,

tropic sun with just enough clouds,

periods of relief,

cooling breezes

DOLPHINS

A thrill ride at sea to watch dolphins in their natural habitat

beats seeing them perform in unnatural enclosures.

This old man held on through the bone-rattling transport.

Never was one for carnival rides.

But oh! the joy on younger faces

far surpassed any discomfort on an old man's part.

KAMIKAZE

While everybody swims, I sit and watch

a graceful bird make circles in the air.

She dives, a kamikaze pilot,

into the water between bathers

and comes up just as fast, a small fish in her beak.

Moments later, she does the same

again and again and again.

SUNDAY IN MARTINIQUE

*** **Morning** ***

Church bell tolls the hour,

echoing through green hills and down

to bathers in the bay

who do not know the Angelus

but float among multi-coloured fish and turtles.

Peaceful hum of happy tourists

escaping rain and winter cold.

✷ ✷ ✷ **Noon** ✷ ✷ ✷

Boom box booms.

Tiny tots escape their keepers' ties.

Buckets and spades

dig bathtubs in the sand.

Grandpa sits content 'neath parasol,

happy to observe the gifts

he once enjoyed.

✶✶✶ **Evening** ✶✶✶

Two plus two make six –

one spouse adds to the loving count.

The younger three cavort in briny circle

while adults scuba tropical delights

in lengths of sparkling bay.

Et sur la plage desmoiselles

en robes de soie.

QUELLE PATIENCE!

He leads me gently into water,

step by step until deep enough to dive in.

What pleasure to swim in a warm sea.

Loving hands guide me safely ashore

to sit once more beneath a beach umbrella.

So much love in those strong arms.

AS A FATHER SHOULD BE

My son is instructing my grandson

in the manly art of push-ups.

I never did – teach him, that is.

Push-ups and other rigorous exercises

were part of Navy training.

Enough for me!

Did I not teach him?

Did it not even cross my mind?

Or is it just that I don't remember?

My son is a dad the way dads should be.

Makes me proud.

But in my quavering mind I ask,

What of my accomplishments?

What did I do for him?

DRIVING WITH MY FATHER

In this Caribbean outpost,

Cornwall roads were just like these.

My driving on the left; circles and hairpin turns.

He shouting from the back seat

"For the love of God, slow down!"

He was younger than I am now

but still an old man.

I was the age of my son.

Now I understand how he felt

though I said not a word.

MARTINIQUE RUM

French plantation rum has the bite of a ~~CENSORED~~.

Pure rum made from sugar cane,

drunk from small glasses with a slice of lime

and a sprinkling of cane sugar.

Bang! Bang!

SUMAS LAKE, BRITISH COLUMBIA

December 2021

Sumas Lake was formed by receding glaciers more than 8,000 years past. Just over a hundred years ago, European homesteaders drained Sumas Lake where salmon and sturgeon had fed the Sema:th peoples since 400 years before the time of Christ. By settlers' law, lakes were not land, thus those who sailed them had no say. Waters the First Nations Peoples had long considered sacred, as home to herons, ducks and fishermen, were to be no more. The great draining was seen as *progress*.

And so the Valley farmers grew rich on her black loam with cattle, sheep and chickens kept in long sheds. Fruits, vegetables, saffron and even tulips, blueberries, strawberries, broccoli and other fresh goods thrived in abundance while the Stó:lō, "People of the River", went without.

Nature held back; her day would come and Mother Earth would have her way.

SNOW

Watching snow drift over the driveway

I recall shovelling with pride

so many mornings before we set out

in the car made clean and warm.

How we enjoyed our visits

with winter friends

when we were so in love.

GARDENS

I have known gardens
planted with love –
rockeries, goldfish ponds, lilies and mums.
Roses thrived on tall trellises.
Azalia, rhododendron,
iris at the pond's edge, purple, yellow, rose.
Every spring crocuses, daffodils, tulips
covered the graves of hamsters, pet mice
and cat-murdered starlings.
Dwarf crested ferns.
Did I mention the well-kept lawn?
Scattered snowdrops.
Family and neighbours have shared
raspberries, rhubarb, strawberries and mint,
lavender, beans, sweet peas and corn.
My compost bin where baby potatoes grew.
Clematis purple spray flecked with white
high over the back gate.

Bamboo in half barrels

and some along the fence and onto the roadway

with fox gloves

So many mosses and lichen.

Unlike my neighbour, I knew none of the native names,

even witches hair, speckled horse hair and blood-spattered beard.

STONES & DRIFTWOOD

Stones were always part of my garden.

Shiny pebbles picked with care from a tiny beach

on the north shore of Lake Superior,

beautiful hunks of granite blasted from the Coast highway,

placed with back-breaking care.

Driftwood in extraordinary shapes

harvested from wood-strewn beaches

Sechelt to Davis Bay.

Never imitating other people's gardens.

Always my own creation,

more often wild than organized

including three rabbits, four racoons

and a striped garter snake.

GARDEN PLANTS

The best garden plants are those we grow ourselves

or, at least, plant as seedlings.

Storefront plants in pots don't last.

Too soon, the blooms fade and die.

Only with heroic effort, do some survive.

I still have a poinsettia from two Christmases ago.

Love has kept its scarlet leaves all that time.

THE CULPABILITY OF VALERIA

a story of Mexico

Two American tourists, George and Muriel, were driving their rental car through mountains north of Oaxaca City, Mexico. It was a beautiful Sunday morning.

On a small farm, deep in those same hills where the road wound around high cliffs and steep precipices, Miguel Hernandez and his young wife, Anna Maria, kept two dozen chickens, three pigs, and one ancient milk cow, Valeria. Unfortunately, Valeria tended to wander onto neighbouring farms and sometimes for many miles along the winding mountain road.

Thus it was that on the Sunday in question, George, distracted by the beauty of the valley below, was forced to swerve to avoid hitting Valeria as she suddenly appeared plodding along in the middle of a rather sharp curve.

At the same time, Miguel Hernandez, driving his decidedly dilapidated Ford truck, approached from the opposite direction. The resulting collision left one rental car and one ancient Ford truck in a condition rather the worse for dangling parts.

After 2-1/2 hours of anxious waiting, Constable José Ricardo arrived on the scene. The Ford had obviously been struck while driving on the appropriate side of the road. However, a "suitable" contribution to the police benevolent fund assured George's inculpability.

Meanwhile, according to Mexican law, all persons involved in any kind of motor vehicle accident were to remain secured until appearance before a local magistrate sometime on the following Monday morning. Thus Miguel would spend the balance of the day and that night in the local hoosegow. George and Muriel dined with the chief of police before spending the night in a hacienda; while Valeria became an unwilling guest of the municipal wrecking yard.

By Monday noon, the Americans had been attested innocent victims. Miguel, whose wife Anna Maria made the best tortillas anywhere, had also been judged guiltless. There remained only one party, unable to assert her innocence.

All concerned, including the judge's wife and five children were invited to a roast beef dinner courtesy of Valeria. Thus the appropriateness of Mexican Justice was upheld. The cost of automotive repairs would remain a separate issue.

MY MOTHER'S GARDEN

One year I built my mother a goldfish pond

with waterfall run from a pump, switched at the back door.

Mostly the pump remained silent except when visitors came.

When the door bell rang, she turned on the pump

in case visitors would want to see her waterfall and pond.

My mother still knew her garden and the birds

even when Alzheimers had stolen the rest of her memory.

She knew a rose from a rhododendron.

She no longer knew my name.

I know my love of gardening

comes from my mother's obsessions –

gardening, painting, music.

WARTS AND ALL

My gardens always contained imperfections.

Sometimes I argued with Nature.

She always has the last word and accepts us as we are

"Warts and all"

No matter what, she'd set things right

and mint would creep through greenhouse walls

carrying sweet perfume to greet me as I'd enter.

Nature continues her healing path

and I take comfort in memories of beautiful gardens.

FRIENDS IN MY GARDEN

Tiny frogs the colour of moss

with parallel stripes of bright red or yellow,

red-backed salamander,

Steller's Jay to scold me as I refill the bird feeder

and a junco flying to gather seed

flipped from the feeder by my friend the grey squirrel.

In Sechelt, the deer used to eat my raspberries.

I didn't mind.

There were always enough left for me

and for occasional guests.

I talked to all the animals

and to the birds and fishes in my gardens.

We've never argued.

Often they were my only companions for weeks on end.

MARGOT'S GARDEN

We had rabbits in Margot's garden.

They'd continue munching crocuses

as I walked out in the morning.

Neither of us minded.

My annoyance was with the racoons

that dug up the lawn in search of grubs.

Perhaps they were helping in their own way

by ridding the lawn of pesky larva

but I had to do so much patching.

We never ate the green grapes

but left them to racoons

who happily sat in the bower

munching and not moving

even as we passed through.

Everyone seemed to know their place

in our Crescent Beach garden.

GOLD DUST & BLACK DEATH

A haze of gold dust covers the garden furniture,

smothering the black/grey from

diesel and coal trains, carrying black death

from neighbours in the South East to the

only port in North America willing

to act as way station for Chinese factories.

The gold dust keeps my love inside as it floats by

in Nature's mating season.

It is the black/grey that will end my love's life before her time.

THIS YEAR'S GARDEN

Today, I have a dozen or so pots

on my balcony, on plastic shelving,

sheltered beneath two windows.

Splashes of rain are just sufficient

to keep my garden watered

but not to the point of drowning.

I have no rocks, no driftwood,

not even shiny pebbles,

but a garden just the same.

The miniature roses have survived thus far,

reminding me of the wild roses

along the beach front in Crescent Beach.

I do miss the chickadees

but perhaps the 21st floor is too high for a visit.

BOOZE, BREAKUP AND COUNSELLING

Sitting at a table near the pool players, he was seemingly absorbed in the game but muttering to himself.

"Hi! May I join you?" I indicated the empty chair opposite.

"It's a free country."

I sat in silence, not wanting to intrude on the conversation he was having with himself.

"Goddam unfriendly place!"

Not sure that he was addressing me, I responded. "People are certainly friendly when you get to meet them."

"What the hell do you know about it?"

"Sorry, would you prefer to be alone?"

"No!" He glanced at me. "Let me buy you a beer."

"A glass of dark," I said, knowing that one should never argue with a person in a volatile state.

He came back with a glass of light.

"Thanks," I nodded, indicating "*here's to you*". I took a sip.

He sat in silence.

Then, out of the blue, "She's gone. Just goddam got up and went back to her mother's."

I listened, waiting.

"Her mother is more important than me... always more important than me.... What does she think, I don't count?"

"Family is always important to a mother." I responded, trying to be helpful.

"What the hell do you know about it?"

This was where I came in. "Could I drive you home?" I offered.

"What the hell, do you think I'm drunk?"

Quietly, "No." Further silence.

Then, after giving him time to mull it over, "The police might stop you on the highway and think you're under the influence." Another pause. "Let me drive you home and I could arrange to get you back for your car tomorrow."

He sighed. "I'll be alright, I have a sleeping bag in the truck."

"Well, take it easy," I said, "I have to be getting on home, big day tomorrow."

I wondered what I had almost gotten myself into. As I made my way out I stopped at the bar to suggest that my friend in the corner had had enough for the evening.

"We'll give him some coffee and he'll sleep it off in his truck in the parking lot."

I went home for the night, but couldn't sleep thinking of my acquaintance sleeping in his truck.

In the weeks to come I was to unravel from his reluctant grumbles, bit by bit the marriage that had gone sour.

One day I suggested a new start. "How about if I could get you and your wife to sit at a table and try and solve your differences? I could be there to offer assistance if required. Maybe I could help."

After some weeks, and a private meeting with the wife, I got the two of them sitting at their kitchen table, yelling back and forth.

"Now you're both venting your frustration. That's a good start," I said, trying to offer some encouragement.

Several days later he was taken to hospital. His liver had given out and he was lucky to still be alive. The wife came to help nurse him back to health. After weeks of daily visits and arguments in my attempt to create a positive attitude, he eventually went to Vancouver for "the cure".

The doctor had told him in the hospital that any more drink would prove fatal.

Weeks later, he was back home a new man. He and his wife seemed happy. He was building a workshop in the garage and planning a trip with his wife where they would celebrate his coming birthday.

One day, following an argument, he went in frustration to visit another friend. A few days later, he was admitted to hospital where, on his birthday, he died of sclerosis of the liver.

I felt as if I had won a minor skirmish but he had lost the main battle.

I had also lost a friend.

WE HAUNT THE PAST

The flowers are gone, long gone.

Remember them when you and I

delighted in their fragrances

many a summer afternoon?

On the lawn, the beautiful manicured lawn,

a truck is parked where deer once came to sleep

beneath the Arbutus, rusty red,

matching colours in the autumn mist.

We kissed beneath that weathered limb.

But now you're gone.

Our memories shimmer in the air.

We haunt the past.

I SHALL RETURN

Gardeners are forever young.

I too am a young gardener,

made young by the earth from which we are all made.

My fingers sift through the ashes of countless lives.

One day I shall return

to be part of some other lover's garden.

LISTENING

In Sechelt,

I had no television, no radio and no newspapers.

I had a cat and my many garden residents.

I really learned to listen in those days.

Every now and then I'll stop and listen

to the subtle sounds that surround me.

When we sheathe ourselves with recorded music and electronic speech,

we fail to hear the delicate voices of nature and our inner being.

Sound has something to tell us beyond words.

It's up to us to stop and listen.

That is a path to finding peace.

THE IRIS

In the 12th century, Louis VII took the iris as his symbol,

incorporated into his coat of arms,

the "fleur de Louis" became the fleur-de-lis,

symbol of royalty, power, honour,

grandeur, faith and unity

and the Royal Arms of France.

Used world-wide,

the fleur-de-lis is also featured

on the Coat of Arms of the United Kingdom,

showing loyalty to the alliance between England and France.

PARENTHOOD

How long ago I gave advice

to this same son who now so deftly

guides his own, and me.

But oh, to a degree far better done

than I in my attempts back then

when I was young.

My son acts like the father I never had.

He looks after me but I feel so beneath him.

Is this what old age is all about?

An old man's wit may wander ere he die:

"Idylls of the King", Alfred Lord Tennison.

Are these scribbles the ravings of an old man?

Will they bear meaning for anyone apart from a few stalwart friends?

Much of this I write for family

without knowing what their response might be.

Do some of us write to be read after we're gone?

Or do we write to free us of demons?

GRANDCHILDREN

I am blessed with three beautiful grandchildren.

One is about to choose a university and a whole new life.

I feel her emotions.

To my grandfatherly impression, she is brighter by far than I have ever been.

I'm amazed by her resourcefulness and drive.

She is able to solve problems

that leave the rest of us in quandary and confusion.

Her next few years will determine a bright future.

The choice must be hers alone.

Two others will follow their own path.

I hold my breath for all of them.

They will step where I have never gone.

Some good has come out of my life.

Too many parents and grandparents make the mistake of thinking

that their children and grandchildren

should be as *they* were.

Our children's lives are not ours.

FISH AND CHIPS

a postcard story

Mr. Alfred Pickford-Jones approaches the park table, looking to right and left, to make sure no one else has the same spot in mind. Under his left arm he carries a folded newspaper and a long black umbrella. In his right hand he carries a package, neatly wrapped in newspaper.

Mr. Jones is a tall, thin man in his late seventies or early eighties. He wears a bowler hat, a dark blue raincoat extending to his knees, and thick, horn-rim spectacles that contrast strikingly with his snow white goatee and moustache.

Fastidiously, he circles the table to find a spot that suits him, before he places his package, umbrella, and newspaper on the wooden bench. He draws a large blue handkerchief from his right coat pocket and flicks crumbs from the table. Observing a spot resistant to his efforts, he picks up a twig, scrapes at the table surface, and blows the residue off the table at the far end. The flicking, scraping, and blowing take three minutes at least.

He shakes out his handkerchief with both hands, until a crumb falls, before he deigns to return it to his coat pocket. After that, he opens his newspaper and spreads it on the table. A picture offends his eye. He shakes his head, turns over the paper, and smooths it with both hands in an outward, sweeping motion.

He places the umbrella on the far side of the newspaper, adjusts it until it's perfectly centred, and positions the package precisely opposite the umbrella.

Before he sits down, there is just one more thing he must do. He extracts his handkerchief, dusts the bench, shakes the cloth with both hands as before, and returns it to his pocket.

Gazing in satisfaction at the arrangement before him, he at last sits down, looking to right and left to ensure he's alone. He removes his bowler with both hands, places it carefully above the umbrella, and adjusts it. Just so.

Still far from done, he reaches into another coat pocket and extracts a small biretta cap, patterned in tartan. This he places on his nearly bald head.

At last, Mr. A.P-J. carefully begins to open the package, folding back each sheet of newspaper at a time.

The meal exposed before him at last, he rises to shoo away the gathering pigeons, first to one side, then to the other. Again, he sits down. His handkerchief will serve another purpose now. He tucks it behind his collar and spreads it out as much as he can.

For just a moment, he bows his head in thanksgiving. Then he pulls his sleeves up a notch and commences his meal.

With customary precision, he chews each mouthful twenty times. Occasionally, he breaks off a part of a chip and tosses it to the pigeons, now reassembled nearby, scolding one or two for apparent greed as he does so.

At the close of his meal, Mr. Alfred Pickford-Jones removes his "bib", shakes it out, and returns it to his pocket. Carefully, he folds up the newspaper within the one he used for a table cloth, removes the cap from his head, and replaces that with his bowler hat.

Only then does he pull out his harmonica from his vest pocket and turn away from the table. To serenade the birds.

MISSION

Here live monks who give their lives

to poverty, to chastity, to obedience

and to Christ.

Poverty I have lived.

Chastity, a struggle when young.

Obedience is the hardest act of all.

To submit my will to one

whose judgment I cannot abide,

killing spirit, creativity and grace.

How could one give what is taken?

The poem consumed by flames,

the song unsung,

canvas forever unpainted.

Gifts to be given in joy

are not to be taken in spite

by men who see the devil in the prize.

* * *

That image was in an age long gone.

These men appear peaceful in their choice.

GUILT

I remember

a mother scarred by war

a father I never saw.

Memories of sirens

flashes of light

and death

screaming through the night.

Those nightmares never leave

though we grow old who lived the years of hate.

The poet Patrick Lane has said:

"Guilt is the emotion that wastes a life."

I visit the past.

The past visits me.

Yet I was never really guilty.

I was the victim

and victims are made to feel guilty.

AND A CHILD WILL LEAD

The old men no longer speak of wars long fought.

boasting of honour and shame unvoiced,

battles lost and sometimes won,

wine and beer and cigarettes,

old prejudices and other poisons

of glory and ignominy.

Most companions are long gone

and conversation has turned to saving

what's left of our frazzled globe.

Though dictators and bullies still raise their fists,

a young girl leads with calls

for sober thought and action.

Whole nations move in search of peace

and better lives.

This world ought never be the same.

PRAYER

What happens to all the prayers

I prayed throughout those many years?

Will they still count

when all my time is done

and questions linger still

of where and who and when?

Will someone please answer,

Why?

KARMA

In another life, another time,

driven by memories, fear and shame,

consumed in guilt,

this soul slept homeless,

on the streets of Montreal.

A lifetime passed,

lost, wasted,

a drunken junkie.

What could have been,

unfulfilled into old age

Some spark of faith blossomed

burst into flame.

Destiny is our own making.

There's no one else to blame,

no matter past events nor pain.

THE SHAWL

A Christmas Story

Benjamin was not at all like the other boys in and around Bethlehem. A dreamer, he spent his days talking to imaginary friends. Other children either ignored him or laughed at him. Some even threw stones.

The youngest of five, Benjamin was born without knowing his father. His older brothers, Hevel and Uri, hired out as shepherds, and his sister, Hadar, cleaned and washed bedding for the town innkeeper, while his mother cooked and mended clothes to keep the family together.

The family lived in a small wine-maker's hut on a hill above the valley where healthy grape vines once grew. Nobody ever talked of the father who lived in shame away from those who had once known and loved him as a successful wine maker.

This winter had been the coldest in memory, with nighttime frost and snow on the hills and even in the valley between, where thin sheep grazed.

"Benjamin," his mother called him, "I want you to take this hot lentil soup to your brothers. Stop dreaming and get on with you. Here, take my shawl to keep yourself warm. And don't dawdle on the way."

The boy ran zig-zagging between boulders and leaping over dead olive boughs and twisted vines. Even for Benjamin, it was far too cold for daydreaming. In the valley, sheep wandered between patches of frosty grass and scrub. The shepherds' tent was empty with no sign of shepherds nearby.

He looked to the far side of the valley and up the limestone hill towards Bethlehem where, bathed in an extraordinary light, a crowd appeared to be gathering close to the travellers' inn.

Believing his brothers to be with the crowd, Benjamin left the soup in the tent and went to find them. On his way, he stopped to rescue a tiny lamb caught in brambles and brought it with him, giving it to his eldest brother. Then, past shepherds, travellers and gawkers – including the innkeeper – Benjamin pushed his way into a stable.

He saw and heard a young mother crooning to a tiny baby wrapped only in rough linen, lying amid hay placed to feed oxen and donkeys.

"Poor baby must be cold," he thought. He took the shawl from his shoulders and gently placed it over the baby in the manger.

"Thank you dear child." The mother smiled at him and returned the shawl, wrapping it once more about the boy's shoulders. "You yourself will find the air cold. Your heart alone makes us warm." The mother gave Benjamin a hug and the man who was with her ruffled his hair. Benjamin left happy and excited to talk to his brothers who waited for him outside.

"We have to get back to the herd." Hevel, the older brother, said. "You hurry home or mother will be worried."

Filled with wonder and eager to tell his mother what he had seen, Benjamin raced towards home.

Not far from the edge of town, Benjamin came across a beggar dressed in rags and ringing a little bell. As the boy drew close the beggar waved him away. "Stay away! Unclean! Stay away!"

Benjamin saw that the beggar's face and hand were covered with dark scabs.

The other hand was wrapped, hanging limp.

"Where do you live?" He asked. "You must be very cold." Despite the beggar's protestations, the boy approached and once more taking the shawl from his shoulders, wrapped it around the poor man. The beggar shouted out his thanks as Benjamin skipped off towards home, only looking back once before turning out of sight.

Benjamin couldn't wait to tell his mother about the baby, the warm light that shone from above, and the angel voices that sang to him all the way home.

"You're soaked through you silly child. And where's my shawl? You wicked boy."

With that, Benjamin's mother shook her head and threw her hands in the air. He was beyond hope but still she loved him. Doing the only thing she could, she gathered him tight in her arms.

Just then, the door swung open. There, holding the shawl was the beggar. This time, his face and hands were without blemish. The scabs gone.

Benjamin's mother collapsed in disbelief and tears, then whispered to her son, "Your father has come home."

DISOWNED – DISINHERITED

No sooner had I left, my mother discarded my belongings.

My Navy uniform and all my clothes were gone.

Then she burned my First Nations outfit:

Tasseled doe-skin jacket and pants

and full length moccasins.

Sacred memories.

She couldn't stand the smell.

RULED BY GREED

The gods were content in their Creation

until man began to interfere,

dictating when and how they were to be worshipped,

offering suffering and death

to all who chose alternate paths.

Men and women were hung, burned, drowned and enslaved

who dared differ from the "Truth".

Children have been seized from mothers' breasts

to be "converted" into what they were not.

We make our own Heaven, Hell, Purgatory by the way we live.

Existence is somehow continuous, even after death.

For now, we live on.

HIDDEN

Becoming an adult was exceedingly difficult for me. I missed much of my childhood with war and lies and hidden guilt and so much wickedness in the world. Then my teenage years were a horror of running and hiding and guilt and trying so desperately to please a mother who could not be pleased and a step-father who ignored me at best but hated me even more. The only love available was from the three babies.

I pored mine on them while my stepfather suspected my motives as if I were a deviate.

He set bullies on me in some sort of attempt to turn me into the kind of boy he might have accepted but which I could never become.

And still I searched for the Divine. With my eyes I searched for you but could not find you.

>All this time, You were within me.
>
>You are still here.
>
>Saint Augustine

BIRTH

A memory swirls back as if from another world:

My mother has her legs spread wide.

She's yelling at me to hurry with the towels;

hot water has not yet boiled.

She lifts her behind and I push two towels under her.

She pushes and screams.

I don't know what to do.

"Get the water and more towels!"

I'd never imagined a sight so awful

as that space between my mother's legs.

And the yelling and the noise from outside.

"Where's that bloody midwife?"

"Where's your sister? I sent for her hours ago."

Then the baby's head is showing.

"You'll have to use your hands and pull"

"Did you wash your hands?"

"Go wash them again."

"Hurry up."

"Help me now. Pull!"

and a little sister is born

and then another.

There's a mess of blood and cords and babies.

The midwife arrives in a huff.

"You've done enough! Go to bed."

All the between times are like a film strip viewed too fast.

I lie in bed to the sounds of babies crying

and a woman's voice far too loud.

Next morning, our garden shelter is flattened

by buzz bomb shrapnel.

VALCARTIER,
QUEBEC

My sister and I dove, panicked, into ditches when planes flew out from Valcartier.

Adults laughed at us, initially, then punished us for "putting on a show".

No one understood our fear as machine guns rattled in our memories.

Not so long before, on our way to school in Sussex, we had been strafed by monsters from the sky.

It takes time to lose the fear of war.

VICTIM

Victims wear a sign on them that says, "Beat me up. I'm a victim."

How many times was I set upon by bullies out on a drunk?

In Victoria, as a member of the Royal Canadian Navy, I was Akela to a cub pack. I loved working with the kids but wearing a cub-master uniform off base was not a good idea for any sailor on a Saturday night. Returning home, I was set upon, stripped and dumped head first into a garbage barrel. My cub-master uniform disappeared.

Rescued from that ordeal, I spent a week in hospital while nose and fingers mended and my eyes gradually reopened. I continued with the cubs but dressed as everyone else when leaving base.

I would still be beaten up from time to time by drunken sailors.

I didn't drink; never had the money.

What was it about me that attracted bullies?

Newly arrived in Canada in 1945, I dressed and spoke funny. Before long, I also smelled of pee. When I wet the bed, which became increasingly more frequent, there was no time to shower. We had only one bathroom.

I lived with my shame and like a wounded chicken, attracted constant abuse.

Is a victim permitted to ask *why*?

WAR AND HEALING

Where was I on September 11th 2001 when the planes crashed into the crystal towers?

I had just completed the first full draft of *The Cameleon Sings* wherein I had revisited childhood horrors with startling flashbacks in my "Healing Garden". Four publications later, that story would become *Discovered in a Scream*.

Such contrast between glass towers and healing gardens. While grief-crazed Americans called for revenge and the world licked its way to the addiction of war, I found continued healing with Margot, the love of my life.

With the span of time, is it permitted for an old man to suggest that healing gardens be employed by the leaders of nations?

Then there is the problem being faced by our one and only healing garden in all the Universe.

Planet Earth.

EARLIEST MEMORIES

Among my earliest memories before the war.

Paul Robeson, Noel Coward and countless parties

with my mother at the piano.

Raunchy songs and limericks. Mother loudest of all.

Soft loving songs with Paul Robeson.

My mother did an oil painting of Paul Robeson holding a clarinet.

After her death, my stepfather got rid of that painting

and one she had done of me in sailor uniform.

A past he wanted to forget.

What had she brought back from the war that he needed to obliterate?

My sister and I were among those ghosts of wartime misadventure.

Naomi died too soon of cancer.

I survived, disowned.

And that's another story.

REMEMBERING AND LETTING GO

It is only in remembering the past

and learning its truths

that we can live in the present

and let the past go.

A WARTIME STORY

AND ITS CONSEQUENCES

We had been quite happy living on our small farm in Finchingfield, Essex.

Then our barn was incendieried during an air raid and we were suddenly living with our uncle in London, Mother worked in a sausage factory and she hated it. The other workers called her Mrs. Lah-de-dah. She'd never had to work before.

Next, she was out at all hours, especially at night, driving an ambulance, then motorcycle dispatch. Then, without warning, Naomi and I were sent off to boarding school and we were miserable.

One day, on a visit from our mother, we innocently asked "When is Daddy coming home?"

"Your father's dead and that's all there is to it."

Only many years later did I learn the truth.

When was it? Naomi and I were kidnapped from boarding school and kept in a barn until a scout troop on a weekend camping trip found us.

Who was it that delivered us to another boarding school much stricter than the first until, following a major disaster at school, we were finally sent back to live with our uncle in London?

Mother was no longer there and we weren't to ask.

What terrible fear led my mother to abandon my father, a prisoner of war in North Africa, marry a French Canadian officer

These are all memories we were told to forget. None of this ever happened.

Finally, after not hearing from our mother for such a long time, Naomi and I were sent to live with her in Broadbridge Heath, Sussex. By that time, she was quite pregnant and always angry. For more than a year and a half, Naomi and I were forbidden from speaking to anyone. We were not permitted or were unable to take the school bus but had to walk miles to and from school in Horsham, in all weather, along country roads frequented by army lorries, motorcycles and jeeps carrying loud Canadian and American soldiers. However, none of our questions were ever answered.

In Sussex, after the twins were born early in March 1944, we were all four taken into Horsham where we were baptized into the Catholic Church by the Bishop of Horsham. Naomi and I had received almost no instruction to prepare.

Both our names were changed. My name went from Bendt Holger Nuttall-Smith to Benoit Joseph Boucher. Naomi kept her first name. We were not to mention our old names – ever!

Only in my fifties did I find my "dead" father alive and well in an Anglican Franciscan monastery in London. He had been taken prisoner in North Africa, ended up with Bedouin in the desert and released quite long after the war had ended. He returned to England to find us gone "without a trace". After many months of searching, my dad gave up and went to work with the black dock workers in London's East End.

With my father and the recovery of my name, I found an entire family: an elder sister, an aunt and eight uncles. Both grandparents had died some time after the war.

***

My sister Naomi died in the Lachine General Hospital very close to where I was teaching.

Hospital staff had been given strict instructions that I was not to be permitted to see her. Only on the day of her death was I allowed in to say goodbye.

What had she learned that I was not to know?

Sadly, we had become strangers from the time I left for the Navy. She had joined the Wrens the following year using her birth name. Somehow we never connected.

Our teen years in Quebec had been fraught with constant anger from our mother. Apart from household chores which were to be done in silence, and taking turns baby-sitting three little sisters, we each found our own friends, she more successfully than I. Still, we both shared a fairly equal diet of blows with wooden spoons, pots and pans, and other punishments as well as distrust from a stepfather who preferred to stay clear from household turmoil.

In winter, we were often locked out of the house even on the coldest days. Naomi usually had friends she could visit.

I had very few real friends as I was the *"maudit bloke"* attending a French school. With only a handful of English speaking friends, I was often without companions whose homes I could share. At school, I was having to explain my clumsiness at running into doors and falling down stairs. Many nights I spent sleeping in the cellar for having done or not done something or other.

Despite all this, I did fairly well in school, even heading my class in French.

However, this made me *"le petit pet"* and brought on more black eyes and cut lips.

Never having seen a dentist, two front canines stuck out in a jagged jumble only to be removed upon joining the Navy.

In the spring of my ninth grade, my stepfather sent me to work on a farm, as "education was being wasted on one who would never amount to anything". My meagre earnings were to pay towards room and board at home, which I was never able to pay in full.

June 1950, fighting broke out in Korea.

Having just turned seventeen, I decided to join the Navy but had to have my stepfather's permission to enlist. Permission granted, but a meagre $9 a month was left me, as the rest was allotted to my parents to help pay old debts.

A year later, Naomi was able to obtain her birth certificate from London and join without our parents knowing.

I couldn't have done the same (even if I had thought of it) as I was born in Tanganyka and that country was in the midst of becoming Tanzania. It would be many years before I'd obtain my birth certificate from that African nation.

We may be individuals, but the weaving of events from around the world does effect our lives.

THE SECRET

Disowned several times over the ensuing years, I was surprised when my mother called me up insisting on seeing me right away. My stepfather was not at home so we were to be alone.

This is what I remember my mother telling me:

"Benoit, I have what they call early-onset dementia, which means I will soon not be able to tell you any of this. Papa Francois is not to know and what I am about to tell you must never be repeated to anyone, even after I'm gone. Do I have your promise?"

I nodded enthusiastically and told her, "I promise."

And I have kept my word all these years. Since all participants are now deceased, records from the Special Operations Executive, SOE, were recently released to the archives in London and I feel free at last to tell this never before told story. I desperately wanted to find out more from the records but they were conveniently destroyed in a fire shortly after the war.

Much later I was able to confirm the history. Although Denmark was to remain officially neutral in the war, Germany had invaded and even destroyed the Danish Airforce. Denmark still had a small army and a navy but remained officially inactive. Danes living on the eastern islands resented the German occupation, whereas people living close to the German border tended to be more cooperative with the invaders.

My mother spoke in hesitant clusters of thoughts. She had to drag her memories from behind long-fortified barriers. It was an arduous, dramatic extraction.

"I have to tell you why I had to leave you and Naomi with your Uncle Siegvard all through the London bombing." She tried to connect with my eyes. "And I think he did things to you that you have not told me."

Siegvard was my mother's elder half-brother.

I shook my head apprehensively but said nothing. She was touching on something I had always denied and would bury deeply for years to come.

"I didn't want to leave you but I couldn't keep you and you were no longer safe in boarding school."

Flash-backs of my sister and me being kidnapped left me breathless.

She continued. "I went to work for a special group in London." She paused again, organizing what she wanted to say in her now-fuzzy mind.

"First, as you might remember, I drove an ambulance. Then a… a motorcycle… dispatch. Those weeks in the worst of the bombing were quite exciting. Then, because I have always been quite fluent in several languages, I worked in the censorship office, reading letters in French, German, Italian, and of course, Danish."

Another pause. "When the War Office had checked police and other records, I was told to go to 64 Baker Street in London. I remember that. Then I was sent to a country house – can't remember the name… And then to a place called Arisaig House in Scotland for some pretty rigorous training. We did, we did so many bad things. There were men and women from so many European countries…"

Mother had to constantly stop to search for words. Sometimes she'd repeat herself. At other times, she'd forget where she was in the telling.

"Eventually, they told me I was to be sent into Denmark and, although my own mother wouldn't have me, I would get to be with my half sisters as if I had never left. There, I would be contacted by the Danish underground."

Mother stopped and was silent for several minutes as she tried to recall details.

Then she recovered her train of thought.

"Things happened in Denmark that I can't even tell you now although I am breaking the War Secrecies Act which I had to swear to on pain of years in prison. So you must never tell anyone else what I am about to tell you, yes?" Her eyes focussed on me again, intently. I nodded.

Here followed another period of awkward silence as if she was reconsidering whether to tell me or not. Mother regained her tenacity to tell me her secrets.

"My assignment was to go to my family in Denmark. I only remember being revoltingly sick most of the night in a little fishing boat that dropped me off at Nordby on the west coast of Denmark. It was the worst day at sea I have ever spent." She shivered hard, thinking of it.

"I don't know how, but the person who was to meet me was there waiting on shore, at night, just like they planned. She took me across Denmark, mostly in the dark. I never heard from her again." Mother sighed and I allowed her more time to organize her thoughts. "There were plans. In Denmark, I could not confide in anyone… It was dreadful."

Mother found her resolve to carry on. "My family lived in Svendborg. My younger half-sister was attending classes in Odense, about 46 kilometres from home, so she stayed with some friends close to school. This was long before that city had a university and I don't remember what Katrine was studying at the time. I only remember that Odense was the home of Odin of the Vikings. Perhaps she was studying history. Odense was also the birthplace of Hans Christian Anderson. Anyway, Katrine and her friends were planning to visit some place or other by bus… I think they were part of a singing group that used to get together to sing Danish songs, remembering the 1864 war with Germany and to boost national pride during the occupation."

Mother looked at me as if she wanted to hold my hands but something, even then, held her back from showing affection.

She shrugged. "I told her to ride her bike because I knew something was about to happen but, of course, couldn't tell her what. It was raining and my sister argued with me but she and her friends did ride their bicycles and the bus they would have taken was blown up by the *Den danske modstandsbevægelse* – the Danish resistance."

Mother wrung her hands, wishing she could change what happened. "Whenever an SOE or Resistance event was successful, the Nazis punished anyone they got their hands on."

She shook her head of the memories. "Several lives were saved but my name came up eventually and so I was blamed for others dying and for those who were rounded up and shot."

Although Mother had not yet told me what she was doing in Denmark, she had been on a roll and I listened attentively without interrupting or asking questions. But now she had come to a halt. I leaned in close, without touching her.

"I have told you too much. I had things to do and there was more danger than I'd ever been in until then." Again, her hands started toward mine but drew back.

"Eventually I was to be taken by the Resistance to Copenhagen, then to Helsingor and by fishing boat to Sweden and back to England. But even in England, we were no longer safe. Then I met Papa François… and I can tell you no more." Her body collapsed inward with the ordeal of speaking with me so plainly.

The next time I saw my mother, she was in an Alzheimer's hospital. She no longer recognized me and the story she had told me at Lac Sir John had slipped from my mind.

DEALING WITH A QUIZLING

> Author's note: while everything else in this book is as accurate as I can make it, this one story is fully fiction!

Alice was to "eliminate" a quizling, whom only she could get close to.

As a young girl, Alice, my mother, had been sent first to a rather strict boarding school in Amiens, France. Not getting on very well at school, she was sent to live with a couple in Sonderborg, a little over 200 kilometres by road from her home in Svendborg, although the relationship had never been explained.

Finding his "niece" rather a handful, Onkel Edvard sent Alice to a convent boarding school in Hanover, Germany from which she was also expelled. Continuing her contrary ways, on a dare Alice had crawled under benches in chapel to discover what the nuns wore under their habits. She was caught and sent home much to her shame but secret delight.

What did the nuns wear under their habits? Mother never said.

Onkel Edvard wasn't really an uncle – just a friend of Alice's mother. He visited when mother was a little girl. "He sort of liked little girls."

Anyway, this was all within the context of the fraught politics in Denmark at the time. Onkel Edvard turned out to be a known anti-Semite (a rarity in Denmark) and a rather high-ranking member of the pro-Nazi National Socialist Workers' Party of Denmark (NSWPD). He was, amongst other things, helping the leader, Frits Clausen, to plan the eventual dispatch of Danish Jews to Nazi concentration camps, despite King Christian X objecting forcefully to German deportation plans and the strong support of the Danish Freedom Council.

In late 1941, when the Danish foreign minister, Erik Scavenius, visited Berlin, German authorities insisted Denmark choose not to avoid its "Jewish problem". A Danish anti-Semitic newspaper used these statements for an attack on the country's Jews. Then arsonists set a fire at the Great Synagogue in Copenhagen. The fire was put out with very little damage occurring and Danish courts imposed stiff fines and jail sentences on the responsible editors and arsonists. Denmark's punishment of anti-Semitic crimes during the occupation were a signal to German authorities in Denmark not to mess with Denmark's Jews. Counter to that, countless young Danes were members of the NSU (National Socialist Youth), the DNSAP's youth organization, while thousands of Danes fought in the *Waffen- SS* during the war.

When a roundup of all Danish Jews was eventually called for in September 1943, Danes were united in finding hiding spots, and fishermen volunteered to move several thousand to safety in Sweden.

Most of Denmark's Jews lived in or near Copenhagen, only a short sea voyage from neutral Sweden (typically 5 to 10 km over sea). Only some 470 were eventually rounded up and sent to the *Theresienstadt* concentration camp in Czechoslovakia. In all, over 99% of Denmark's Jewish population survived the Holocaust.

Although Alice's Onkel Edvard was an important target for elimination by the Allies, he was far from the only one the Danish Resistance and the Allies needed to eliminate. The list was extensive.

For now, only the most dangerous were to be immediately targeted, notably Frits Clausen, leader of the 22,795 Danes, registered members of the Danish Nazi Party, the "DNSAP".

With many Danes supporting the Nazi cause, utmost secrecy for any resistance was absolutely crucial.

It was almost impossible to know whom to trust and Alice had already slipped up in Odense. As a result, she would soon be on the DNSAP wanted list. Alice would need to act fast and disappear even more quickly.

Her job was to visit with her "uncle's" family, find out all she could of immediate plans and eliminate the target, a task only she could accomplish.

Onkel Edvard was a somewhat boastful man and did not hide his allegiances. Conversation at meal times frequently turned to the war, the stupidity of the English and turmoil in Britain since the recent arrival of the even stupider Americans.

"Even the English don't like them. Siegvard had worked in Hollywood, California and would definitely be glad to be away from there, although what he's doing in England is beyond me."

The promise was that Hitler would rescue Europe and the world from the Jews and the Communists, the homosexuals and the gypsies. Japan was also assuring that China would not be permitted to overrun the Far East.

"Russia will be defeated and we'll all be far safer, especially those of us on the Baltic. Thanks to Herr Hitler, the world will soon awaken to a new dawn."

Day after day, Alice listened to the diatribe but learned nothing of Nazi plans for the Jews of Denmark.

On occasion, Alice was able to accompany her uncle and aunt's maid, Helga, on shopping trips for groceries and household supplies.

As she waited in the morning sunshine on one such excursion, a young girl bumped into her, uttered, "Undskyld mig," [*Excuse me*], and sneaked her a small package, which she immediately slipped into the top of her panties.

The package, opened in the privacy of the family toilet, contained a brief note: "Ikke et øjeblik at være spildt." [*Not a moment to be wasted*] and a small bottle unmarked.

The bottle contained Potassium Cyanide. Alice knew what she had to do and she had to act fast.

Every night before bed Helga was tasked with bringing her employer a glass of warm milk which he would take with a small glass of his own home-made aquavit.

Alice had a hell of a time convincing the maid to let her do the honours this one night. Finally, an offer of twenty kroner did the trick. Since the Danish Kroner was now tied to the German Deutsche Mark, Alice was almost happy to let it go. Of course, Helga must never let the exchange be known or it would cost her her job.

Alice knocked at her uncle's door.

"Kom ind." [*Come in*]

"Hvor er Helga?" [*Where's Helga?*]

"Helga wasn't feeling well. Besides, I wanted the honour and the chance to thank you for a beautiful visit. I have certainly enjoyed our intimate conversations although I won't pretend I agree with all you say. I have learned enough to respect your right to express your beliefs in your own home. If I pretended to agree past that, you're much too intelligent and already know me too well to accept such a lie."

Onkel Edvard tilted his head as he stared at Alice.

Above the bed hung the portrait of Adolf Hitler and on the bedside table was a picture of Onkel Edvard and Tante Terese from their wedding day, as well as another picture of a young man in Waffen-SS uniform.

Alice put the two glasses, the chilled aquavit and the warm milk next to an empty saucer, possibly used as an ash tray. Then she gave her uncle a quick hug.

As she turned to leave, a ginger cat she hadn't noticed before jumped onto his master's bed.

The story of the dead cat echoed through the house the following morning.

Alice was already gone. Within the hour, Gestapo were everywhere and Helga had been arrested. Tante Terese announced "Never did trust that girl," while household servants stood around in amazement.

Onkel Edvard had driven by car into Germany to the Hamburg-Altona airfield to be flown to DNSAP Headquarters in Copenhagen.

The search was on for Alice. Alice had gone straight to the fishing docks but police were already everywhere with NSU (National Socialist Youth) assisting in the search.

Sheltering near a school, Alice saw a young girl on a bicycle approach her. "Here, take my bicycle and my school books. Go to Tandslet, it's the Lutheran Church, and speak to the youth præst. He will hide you until the coast is clear. Now hurry."

At the church, a harried older man in black clerical dress with ruffled collar found the bicycle parked at the door with Alice inside the church.

He shook his head. "Here's a muddle we'd hoped to avoid. Edvard Schmidt was shot by an assassin before getting to the German border. The entire force is out with roadblocks everywhere. Countless suspects are being rounded up. You will have to stay here. There's no way to get you out."

No sooner had the old man spoken than three Danish policemen entered the church and approached Alice. "Please come with us, Miss Weber."

Escape seemed futile so Alice went with the three men and was placed in the back seat of a police car. She was not handcuffed but the two-tone siren sounded as they drove off.

Instead of to police headquarters, Alice was taken to the Schmidt house where she was to be questioned by (of all people) Tante Terese.

She was not as severe as Alice was expecting. "Tell me, Alice. What have you gotten yourself into and why? You may as well be honest with me."

Tante Terese nodded to the three policemen. "Tak. Du må gerne gå. Jeg tager den herfra." [*Thank you. You may go. I'll take it from here.*]

Alice had no explanation to offer her aunt. She could have made some excuse or other but could no longer think straight.

Her aunt took over the conversation: "I never did like the direction your uncle was taking and I'm not terribly upset that he's gone. But why you?"

Alice had no reply. She'd been ordered to keep silent no matter what, but this was different.

"I must tell you, Helga will be tortured and, no matter what she says, she will die. I have already spoken on your behalf and assured the DNSAP that you were merely visiting and had nothing to do with your uncle's death. I have known for quite some time that there was more than aquavit and warm milk going on with those nightly visits. I'm not unhappy to see him gone and she will pay. Your name came up but only because you were in the house when the attempt was made on your uncle's life. She will surely try to blame you but she will not be believed. And she knows no one in the resistance. She has always been openly supportive of the DNSAP and even joined the National Socialist Youth as a volunteer leader. All this, I'm sure, to curry favour with Edvard. She will die by the very poison she so willingly helped spread."

Tante Terese rang for tea. "You will have to stay here until all this blows over. There will be hostages and I'm afraid your name will not be popular for a long time to come." She glanced up at the ceiling.

"Pity the cat hadn't died sooner."

CLOSING THOUGHTS

As one's life nears its ending,

it should be comforting to know

the world's somewhat better for

a life well lived in love and generosity.

Frailties understood,

strife forgiven,

disagreements resolved,

happiness produced,

love nurtured.

Some strive for fame,

others for heaven, karma, rebirth.

I shall just have to wait and see.

What will be, will be.

AFTER I'M GONE

My ashes will be placed in a container and kept in a niche

in a wall at the Gardens of Gethsemane

and no one will ever visit me there.

We spread Margot's ashes at sea as she had wished.

A very touching and meaningful ceremony.

Close family and many friends were there.

I have great respect for the way First Nations disposed of their dead.

Bodies were exposed on a platform for the return to nature.

Then the bones were collected and moved to a burial site.

The circle of life carries on.

....

Other Titles by
Ben Nuttall-Smith

All available through Rutherford Press

https://rutherfordpress.ca

Margot: Love in the Golden Years, ISBN 978-1-988739-39-7

Discovered in a Scream, ISBN 978-1-988739-38-0

Mad God of the Toltecs, ISBN 978-1-988739-31-1

Crescent Beach Reflections, ISBN 978-1-988739-04-5

Flying With White Eagle, ISBN 978-0-9951743-2-0

Henry Hamster Esquire, ISBN 978-1-988739-07-6

Grandpa's Homestead, ISBN 978-1-988739-47-2

Rhyming Fun With Billy and Trish, ISBN 978-1-988739-51-9

www.ingramcontent.com/pod-product-compliance
Lightning Source LLC
Chambersburg PA
CBHW021450070526
44577CB00002B/335